Pull the fire alarm and walk out with the book when everyone evacuates.

Use counterfeit money to buy the book.

Balance the book on your head and walk out.

Using rubber bands, attach a book under each shoe and walk out.

Buy a piece of candy while the book is under your arm. Walk out holding the receipt for the candy.

Put the book in a shopping bag from a nearby clothing store. Put a nicely folded shirt on top of the book.

Throw the book in the air over the detector and catch it on the other side. Do this casually.

Flip through every page of the book looking for a magnetic sensor. If you find one, remove it. Walk out with the book.

Flip through every page of the book, and while you are doing that, read the entire book in the store. Leave the store with the book in your memory.

Put the book in your friend's bag when they are not looking.

Put the book in your bag when no one is looking.

Put the book inside a folded newspaper you are holding in your hand.

Put the book on the floor near the store's entrance. When some-one enters the store kick the book out the door.

Photograph every page of the book with a digital camera.

Seal the book into an envelope that is stamped and addressed. It is a federal crime to open someone else's mail.

Roller skate out of the store with the book in your hand.

Wear a T-shirt with an image of a kitten in a suit. Hold the book away from the T-shirt (they will all be in love) and walk away.

Take the book on Halloween dressed as Dracula.

Take the book on Christmas dressed as Santa Claus.

Have your little brother hold the book as you both exit the store.

With a group of people, have everyone hold the book as you all exit. Who stole the book if ten people are all touching it?

Put the book underneath a baby in a baby stroller.

Cut the store's power supply after the sun has gone down. Exit in the dark with the book.

Bring a fog machine into the store. Exit with the book in the haze.

Put helium balloons in front of all the surveillance cameras in the store and take the book.

Throw the book outside the store through an open window.

Smash a hole in the store's window. Throw the book through the hole.

Put the book inside a super sized soda cup and walk out pretending to drink the soda.

Drop the book in an upside down slightly opened umbrella.

Kindheartedly open the store's door for an elderly person who is exiting. Leave behind them with the book.

Buy the book, photo-copy it, return it for a refund.

Buy the book, read it, return it for a refund.

Buy the book and take it home. Leave it at your house. Return to the store and find a copy of the same book. With your receipt, “return” that copy for a refund.

Flush the book down the toilet inside the store. Collect it from the ocean.

Release a cinghiale in the store. Exit with the book during the commotion.

For the book that you don’t want, that no one should see, throw it into a trash can inside the store. The store will get rid of it for you.

For the book that you want, put it in the trash can inside the store. Collect it from the outside dumpster later that night.

Steal the book from your friend's bookshelf.

Go out the emergency exit with the book.

Put the book in a bouquet of red roses.

Put the book in
a bouquet of white
roses.

Make a birthday present box with a trap door on the bottom. Slip the book into the box.

Hide the book inside a fake rock.

Put the book inside a cake.

Walk in the store holding a big mirror. The employees will be distracted looking at their own reflection. Hold the book behind the mirror.

Fill a bag with the books you want. Make it heavier than you can carry. Ask an employee to help you carry it outside.

Put the book inside
an empty cereal box.
Glue the box shut
inside the store.

Place a newspaper or magazine (that you brought into the store) on top of the book. Pick up the newspaper or magazine holding the book underneath it. Walk out.

Wearing a coat, put the book under your arm inside your coat.

Put the book you want near the door. Come back later in the day. Enter the store, grab it, and immediately walk out.

Set off a bright flash in the store. Exit while everyone's sight is adjusting.

Set off explosives in the store to make a loud noise. Exit as they go off.

Steal the book with a bloody nose.

Cover the book in thinly sliced mortadella and walk out.

Yell "shoplifter!" and point to someone. When everyone looks, walk out with the book.

Cook up some garlic
in olive oil in the store.
Exit with the book
while everyone is
caught in the ecstasy
of the aroma.

Give all the employees in the store LSD. When they are peaking, exit with the book.

Put the book inside
a bag of Japanese rice
that you happen to
be carrying with you.

Unplug the store’s detection device by pulling the cord out of the electrical socket. Walk out with the book.

Step in dog poop and drag your feet through the store. When people begin to notice the foul smell, make your exit with the book.

Ask your friend to streak through the store. Exit with the book while everyone is distracted.

Call your friend with your cell phone and read them the book.

Copy the entire book by hand in the store.

If the alarm goes off
when you walk out
make a coughing noise
louder than the alarm.

Bring a stapler and a paper bag into the store. Put the book in the bag and staple it shut. No one will question a stapled bag.

Steal the book one page at a time from different stores.

Dress up as a cop and walk out of the store holding the book.

Tie the book to a dog and walk the dog out of the store.

Steal the book
looking like a tree.

Crumple up the book and mark some pages with a pencil so it looks like you have been reading it for a while.

Steal the book dressed like Abbie Hoffman.

Organize 50 people to steal books at the same time in the same store.

Organize 50 people to steal books at the same time in different stores.

Walk in the store with one of your own books that you don’t want. Tell the employees that you are holding your own book. Replace it on the shelf with a different book and leave.

Dress like an employee of the store and walk out with the book in your hands.

Steal the book while you are crying.

Steal the book to cure your depression.

Steal the book while the sun is setting.

This is dedicated to PB and MV.

This publication originated in 2011 as a conversation in The Classroom at Printed Matter's NY Art Book Fair. The Classroom is a series of informal events organized by David Senior.

Originally published by Automatic Books in 2013 together with the Italian translation.

This paperback series is edited and designed by Jan Steinbach.

Also available:

FR Comment voler des livres

ES Cómo robar libros

DE Wie man Bücher klaut

IT Come rubare i libri

ZH 携书潜逃的N种方式

GR Πως να κλέψεις ένα βιβλίο

NL Hoe je boeken steelt

PT Como furtar livros

LT Kaip vogti knygas

DA Bogrov

KO 책을 훔치는 완벽한 방법

KA როგორ მოვიპაროთ წიგნები

HE איך לגנוב ספרים

RO Cum să furi cărți

CH Wiemer Büecher chlaut

RU Как красть книги

JP 書店で本を盗む方法

MT Kif tisraq il-kotba

SQ Qysh me vjedhë libra

HI किताबें कैसे चुराते हैं

TR Kitap nasıl çalınır

SR	Kako mažnjavati knjige/Како мажњавати књиге
EE	Kuidas raamatuid varastada
IS	Hvernig hnupla skal bókum
SE	Hur man knycker böcker
HU	Hogyan lopjunk könyveket
NO	Hvordan butikktyveri bøker

MA പുസ്തകങ്ങൾ എങ്ങനെ കടയിൽ നിന്ന് മോഷ്ടിക്കാം

David Horvitz

How to shoplift books